SUCCESS:
WHAT'S FUN GOT TO DO WITH IT?

JOHN HUI

www.paralimus.com

YOUR KUNGFU MIND

www.facebook.com/groups/894845247308326

DESIGN BY KELLY BADEAU
DANCING TROUT DESIGNS, TUCSON, AZ

PRINTED BY CREATESPACE
WWW.CREATESPACE.COM/6428609
AVAILABLE FROM AMAZON.COM AND OTHER RETAIL OUTLETS
AVAILABLE ON KINDLE AND OTHER DEVICES

ISBN 978-0-9978451-0-5

TABLE OF CONTENTS

SECTION ONE
FUN ME: BUILDING A FUN PERSONA

SECTION TWO
FUN LIFE: BUILDING A FUN LIFE THROUGH PRACTICE AND CREATING NEW OPPORTUNITIES FOR FUN

SECTION THREE

FUN WITH OTHERS: INFLUENCING OTHERS WITH FUN LEADERSHIP AND INSPIRING OTHERS TO BE FUN LEADERS AS WELL

FUN ME: BUILDING A FUN PERSONA

CHAPTER ONE

THE FUN APPROACH

When I was in my last year of college, I was given a book by a now great friend of mine because we had similar journeys in search of personal development. The book was *Mastery*, by Robert Greene. I owe a lot of my personal development and growth to him and the book that he lent me.

At the time, I read at the pace of an elementary school kid. I took a reading test and scored one hundred and forty-two words per minute—that is extremely, agonizingly slow. An average college student reads at four hundred words per minute. Whenever I read a book, I would get this burning sensation in my eyes and spend ten minutes reading through the first few pages. It was a frustrating and terrible experience. As much as I wanted to read the book, as much as the book was evidently helpful to me, I couldn't read it efficiently because I read so slow.

I decided to see if I could find a way to read faster. I looked online and found a strategy called "speed reading." I said, "Oh well, why the heck not? If I can improve my reading speed by at least double, I'll be closer to a college student's reading speed."

The program I found claimed it could triple the reader's reading speed by the end of the program, so I bought it. I worked diligently and followed through with the speed reading exercises. When I started the program, I began to read faster, but I couldn't comprehend anything. By the end of the program, I was reading at around eleven hundred words per minute with ninety five percent comprehension. That was almost eight times my original reading speed. I was able to go through book after book, and it was a thrill to read.

After I became a speed reader, I got more excited about reading books—it was finally fun for me. I went on a book reading spree and read twenty two books in one month. I would be sitting in Barnes & Noble in the morning, and all of a sudden it was nightfall and Barnes & Noble was trying to close for the day. I learned that the fun approach to building a fun persona is to take a basic fundamental understanding of the things that you enjoy. Do the hobbies that you love, and find the basics of what you enjoy, the things that really make you happy. The little things you enjoy—they don't even have to be big— can be magnified and spread out across different aspects of life. Maybe you love cooking, for example. You could find a freelance cooking or meal prep position to generate some extra income while participating in a favorite pastime simultaneously, being able to cook and make money at the same time.

When you're doing fun, basic things that you enjoy, you're releasing chemicals in your brain. These chemicals help you de-stress and help make you a happier person in general. As a happier person, you become a more positive person; people around you will notice

> **Once you start becoming aware of what it is that makes life more fun for you, you become more excited about going out and approaching the taks in life in a fashion that is better for you.**

this in you and become empowered to become happier, more positive people themselves. When you finally understand what is fun to you, you empower people around you. You are doing things that you are passionate about, you are more excited about life, you start thinking about things that can excite yourself and others, and you start making a difference in your community.

In order to figure out how to bring more fun into your life, how to be a more fun person, you have to reflect on what you have already done in your life. What were the best times of your life? Your greatest memories? The times where you laughed so hard, you couldn't breathe and fell off the chair? The times where maybe even you shed a tear or two of joy? Hone in on what exactly it is that made these time so special. What is it that you enjoyed so much about these moments? What did you see? What did you hear? Were you out and about socializing? Were you indoors with close friends just enjoying the moment? Who were you with? What kind of people were they? Or were you by yourself having a good time?

Take note of all the positive things that came out of those moments. We all have these enjoyable, important moments in life when the day is one we don't forget, just like the saying, "You just made my day." It takes only one moment of dedicated fun, excitement, and enjoyment to make someone's day, to make someone enjoy their life that much better that day.

We begin to progress towards our approach to fun by thinking about these moments, assessing how they did it, how they made us feel that way, and the effects of it. We can start generating more of these moments once we figure out the basics of what is fun to us. Once you start becoming aware of what it is that makes life more fun for you, you become more excited about going out and approaching the tasks in life in a fashion that is better for you and start tackling problems in life with a fun approach.

As you're going on this journey to figure out your own fun approach, you have to be willing to learn. That is, you have to learn new ways of thinking. Many people associate differently and have different perspectives. It may be challenging at first, but you have to be willing to figure out what works best for you and learn new ways of solving problems in order to have more fun.

Take, for example, how people complain or feel groggy when they get up out of bed on weekdays, even though maybe they had seven to eight hours of sleep or more. They might feel like there's a lot of weight or pressure on them. That's most likely due to the fact that they're not having enough fun in their lives. They're not happy because they repeatedly use the same approach to their tasks. Maybe there's just not enough excitement and energy. It is at this point, in the rut of life, where it is the most difficult for people to learn something new, to learn a new approach. They're so used to the beaten path, that it's just easier to continue down that road. Veering off the path to wade through the grass may be a bit tougher, may offer a little more resistance, but it might be just a little more fun. It might be in that greener grass that they find their true passion.

You must be willing to work a little bit before your body and mind adjust to a more fun and approachable lifestyle. You have to forget the old things, the old ways that may be comfortable or easy but don't work for you any longer. For some, maybe being a bully to others got them the things they wanted. Maybe it gave them the attention that they wanted for a little while. But being mean to people is ultimately going to drive people away. Humans are herd creatures; if we are isolated and we cannot bond with other people, if we're mean to them and we push them away and we isolate ourselves, something inside us starts dying. That is why the most extreme punishment in jail is solitary confinement. A prisoner is kept in complete solitude for an extended period of time, and this isolation starts digging away, eating away at the soul and psyche.

We have to be willing to forget these old habits that might have worked when we were younger, that might have gotten us to where we are now. These old raggedy habits will not take us to the next level of success that we're vying to get to. We have to be willing to repeat some things, to fall down and try again. We must go out of our comfort zones and try even though we might fumble or fail on the first go around. But if you never try, you'll never know.

Even if you're scared, go out and you try a new activity you never thought you would do, like archery tag, for example. You go out there, you have a great time, you're shooting marshmallow arrows at your friends. You get hit and get a bruise; that's not so fun and yet, you're still having a great time. You're giving yourself a chance to have a great experience. Or maybe archery tag isn't for you, but at least now you know to cross it off your list and try something else. We have to be willing to repeat, to go out and try new things and be able to put ourselves in a learning situation that we weren't willing to do before.

> **"We must go go out of our comfort zones and try even though we might fumble or fall on the first go around. But if you never try, you'll never know."**

{ **"HAVE FUN SAVING THE WORLD, OR ELSE YOU ARE JUST GOING TO DEPRESS YOURSELF."** }

DAVID R. BROWER

CHAPTER TWO
MIRROR MAXIM

I will never forget the day when I was coming home from work, reflecting on all I had done that day. I worked very hard and was super productive. I just wanted to sit down, relax, and get the heat off my shoulders. I finally arrived at my apartment—it was so cool and comfortable from the AC. I got myself a nice, big mug of iced tea, grabbed my computer, sat down on my chair, and laid back to relax. I ended up doing some light YouTube browsing and saw on my Recommended Videos bar a video that led me to my future life coach.

After I connected with him, my life coach helped me realize how much I was holding myself back. I was tearing myself down on a day-to-day basis without even noticing it. I would go to work and berate myself for having not yet achieved my dream, that I wasn't even good enough to have that dream. He helped me learn that I don't have to be my own worst enemy. I don't have to go to bed tearing myself up every night or wake up and slapping myself in the face. Instead, I found a way to harmonize with myself. The nagging little voice in my head instead became my biggest cheerleader, my best friend, and that has been one of the most profound shifts in my career and in my life. It has made a huge difference in how much fun I am having on the day-to-day basis.

I realized that being my own best friend came from the ability to discern my own thoughts, to have a flexible thinking pattern, and develop the desire to change. In order to be able to discern your own thoughts, you must pay attention and listen to what you are saying to yourself on a daily basis, on an hourly basis. Catch yourself when you are over-critiquing a thought.

For example, a lot of people immediately criticize themselves when they make a mistake. They might think, "Oh my gosh, I am such a screw up," or "I'm a failure," and that immediately turns them into their own worst enemy. You know yourself the best, and when you feel insecure and unsafe in your own mind, you don't feel safe or confident in the outside world. You lose that connection with the your own vitality and purpose in life.

When we truly listen to what we are saying to ourselves, we can begin to understand what is happening on a day-to-day, hourly, minute-to-minute basis. We can discern what our internal voice is trying to do, be it positive or negative. Many people have reported in various studies that they experience extremely negative self-talk. It seems a common occurrence to be very mean to oneself, and the saying may be true that we are our own worst critic.

However, once we tune in and discern the little thoughts that are being spewed out by the internal voice, we can start to understand where it's coming from. Maybe it's just trying to help us to get to where we want to go to, but in a negative instead of positive way. Maybe that sharp criticism is saying, "Hey, you are not where you want to be. How are you going to fix that?" or "Hey, we're not having enough fun. How are we going to fix that?" It may be so frequent that we have decided to shut it down, suppress it, ignore it and just say, "Yes, I will get to that later." Then we start losing the fun in our lives. We start losing the energy, the excitement, the vitality that drives us, invigorates us, that makes us leap out of bed in the morning.

We need to address that behavior in order to have more fun in our lives and maximize our success. When you are having fun, when you are excited, when you are energized, you leap out of bed. You look forward to the day and do the things you want to get done. You find your own way, your own path to make sure that they happen. In order to change that behavior, we need to create flexible thinking patterns and start tweaking how the internal voice speaks as we start to notice it. When we hear, "Hey, we're not doing the things we want to do. We are not doing as well as we should," ask back as you would a friend or a coach, "Ok, how can I do better than I already am? How can I have more fun than I already am?" When that negativity creeps in, turn it into constructive criticism. You will be surprised at the amount of responsiveness you get back from yourself. You will start to notice that you ask yourself the right questions, that you start looking for positive answers instead of negative answers. When we are able to twist the internal voice and start asking productive questions, we become our own wisest advisor.

We tweak our thinking patterns so that we are able to warm-up and progress toward being our own best friend. As an athlete does, they have to warm-up and they increase their reach just by that tiny amount. The tiniest amount might not seem like much, but it makes the biggest difference on a long-term basis. The world's best athletes compete in milliseconds in races. When you give yourself that warm-up to increase your thinking flexibility, you give yourself the extra few inches, the extra few centimeters that you need to take over your own mind and become your own best friend.

Once we are warmed-up and once we start asking questions to our internal voice, "How can I be stronger than I already am? How can I do more than I already am doing? What steps can I take to improve myself?" we start to challenge our mind, and we begin to exercise thought flexibility. This allows us to practice something called "success internal alchemy," which is the ability to reframe everything that happens as either a winning experience or a learning experience. This frame of mind exercises the muscle in our brain that allows us to overcome obstacles and challenges and stand back up every time we get knocked down. Utilizing thought flexibility and challenging the critiques of the internal voice becomes more and more natural. We can then, just like an athlete does, go faster and faster once we start practicing.

At first the exercise might be strenuous and clunky, but as you keep going, as you keep challenging, as you keep working at it, you become more and more proficient,

> • **How can I be stronger than I already am?**
>
> • **How can I do more than I'm already doing?**
>
> • **What steps can I take to improve myself?**

and the flexibility and positivity starts to become a part of you. You learn to make friends with yourself. You learn to find solutions in life. You learn how to challenge the obstacles and how to find your own solutions without bringing yourself down.

Then, like after every good work out or exercise, the athlete has to stretch to maintain their abilities for the long run. When you challenge yourself, it's going to be a lot of work, a lot of strenuous activity, so be sure to allow yourself time to stretch, to relax, to sit down for a little bit at the end of the day and reflect on all the things you are grateful for. Think about the amazing achievements you have made throughout the day, the little things from washing the dishes, doing the laundry, taking out the trash to the bigger things like finishing a project, working with the team, and making someone smile.

These are all incredible exercises that you can build upon. Allow yourself to be liberated and think differently whenever a critique comes up in your mind. Create solutions instead of problems. Focus on the beautiful opportunities in your life instead of dwelling on the ugly problems. Consider all the things that you are already doing well and what else you could do to become your own best friend.

Exercising a flexible thinking pattern is ultimately fueled by a desire to change. When your interval voice begins critiquing, telling you, "I don't like this. I need to change," or "Something is not right in my life right now," it is our responsibility to our own integrity as well as to the people we love and the people we impact to notice that problem and

figure out how to change it. We may not realize it, but how we behave impacts everyone around us and impacts our loved ones. When you are not having fun, when you have an internal problem, when you are clashing with yourself and aren't happy, that reflects in your emotions, attitudes, and behaviors. It impacts everyone around you. Your attitude is reflected in your behavior: how you communicate with others, the amount of aggression you show, the amount of irritation you have at your co-workers. All these things stem from a problem in your internal dialogue, and if you don't have the desire to fix that, then you are causing harm to everyone that you love.

Developing the desire to change is a result of realizing the fact that you are not where you want to be. Acknowledging that fact allows you to own it and move a step forward, take that awareness to the next level and improve your current situation.

After developing the desire to change, you must take action. Proceed towards your goal. Take a first step—a class or an intro lesson. Once you take that first step, that first action, you announce to yourself that you care about yourself: "I am going to take care of you because you take care of me." That is when the bond with you and your internal voice really starts to form, and the negative self-talk finally starts going away. Solutions instead of problems are created. The people in your life start noticing your improved productivity, your improved happiness. When we are bonded with ourselves, when we are our own best friend, we feel connected to the world. We increase our productivity. We positively influence the people around us, increasing their productivity. We help people change their states of mind and improve their relationship with themselves simply be being in proximity.

Take that first step and listen to your thoughts, discern where they are coming from. Address the issue and then warm-up to it. Ask questions on how to improve or take the next step, and start exercising the thought flexibility. Then realize that every critique comes from a desire to change and instead of dwelling on the negative, we can take the action to fix it and become our own best friend, one action at a time.

"JUST BE YOURSELF AND HAVE FUN."

RICHARD LOWE

CHAPTER THREE
UPON CLOSER INSPECTION

I remember when I was just a year and a half old, my family and I lived in Taiwan. I often went outside and played. Our neighbor had a black Pomeranian, a very fluffy, very tiny dog. It had small teeth and yapped a lot—not a dog many people would feel threatened by. But when you are a toddler, about 2 feet tall, a Pomeranian is about half your height. I was very intimidated by our neighbor's dog because every time I would walk by, he would bark at me, which I took as a sign of aggression. I didn't realize that he was actually excited to see me and just wanted to play. Instead, I took up a twig to defend myself against this black Pomeranian as best I could.

As the Pomeranian approached me, believing we were about to play fetch, I whacked it in the face with my twig. I hadn't known what I was doing; I was simply defending myself from what I thought was an attack. It was a small, thin twig, but the hit surprised the dog, and he decided I was an enemy. Out of shock, the black Pomeranian nipped me on the calf. Pomeranians' bites don't hurt all that much, but fear overtook me and I started running. I kicked the dog away and started running for home. From then on, that black Pomeranian and I were no longer friends.

I am sure there has been some emotional or painful experience in your life that is disturbing to recall. When you think about the incident, you most likely only consider it from one perspective. Especially if it's very emotionally painful and attached to us, we have difficulty letting that perspective go. That experience might become a sinkhole for the fun in our lives. It makes us less productive. It slows us down. It makes us not want to move as fast as we usually do.

It is critical that we take a step away from that perspective, take a step back from the situation. Picture the situation in your mind and make it smaller, a little more distant and look at it from another angle. Turn it around and reconsider. If I was the Pomeranian and I was really excited to see this little boy that was almost my size, I would want to run up and play with him, too. And when he hits me with a twig, I would naturally want to defend myself. I would communicate, "Hey, I'm not someone to be messed with. I thought we were cool, but I guess not." I would assert some dominance and strike back, just like he did.

When we reconsider the perspective, it takes a lot of effort to do so because we are so emotionally attached to our own perspective. When we picture that image in our mind of the situation, making it smaller and creating some space, that gives us a little bit of emotional advantage. Then when we spin it around and look at the situation from the other person's point of view, we get to see a different perspective. Maybe they did not mean to hurt you? Maybe they were after something else you perceived it as an attack?

We are given the power to transcend the scenario and consider things that have happened to us from all angles. With some effort, we can rewire our own emotional responses to events. Most of us have gotten so good at being uncomfortable that we use this in the wrong way. We use this emotional patterning technique to condition ourselves to get up out of bed every weekday and go to work at a job that might be very trivial and boring, yet we continue to doing the same thing over and over. We allow ourselves to become a numb to the hatred of being stuck where we don't want to be; we pattern ourselves in a calm state when we actually feel extremely punished. Being aware of this blight that is taking over our lives, that is instilling so much inactivity amongst people today, allows us to take that one step further and realize we don't want this pattern in our lives. We don't want to be comfortable at being uncomfortable.

Take that angst and sleepiness of emotions out of your life so you can fight for what you truly deserve: happiness. Fight for the things that you enjoy, the things that excite you and motivate you. Fight for the fun in your life, and do the things that you want to do more often rather than conditioning yourself to tolerate feeling horrible. Envision what is going on when you are patterning yourself, when you say, "Payday is tomorrow. Everything was worth it," when you would much rather be somewhere else, doing something else, seeing someone else, saying something else and enjoying life the way that you have wanted, regardless of the paycheck.

> **Fight for the things that you enjoy, the things that excite you and motivate you. Fight for the fun in your life.**

"PEOPLE RARELY SUCCEED UNLESS THEY HAVE FUN IN WHAT THEY ARE DOING."

DALE CARNEGIE

CHAPTER FOUR
DARING GREATLY

In high school, I was not the most social creature on the planet. In fact, I shied away from social interactions and kept to myself quite a bit. This made it very difficult when it came time to find a date for senior prom. My parents had been encouraging me to attend senior prom, but I really didn't have any interest until I realized that this was my only opportunity to attend something like this since I was graduating high school soon. I decided I would find a date and attend senior prom. The process of finding a date was actually quite challenging because I hadn't had much experience with relationships yet. I was hesitant to ask my potential prom date because she appeared to be a very popular person and, in fact, had already been approached by other people with the same question. It was very daunting to me to even fathom the idea of asking her and having the guts to face the rejection when it came.

In my head, I had already failed fifty times before I mustered up the courage to plan my strategic approach and ask her. I had decided to get up one early morning and walk several miles to her house and ask her to prom before she even got on the school bus. However, I failed to check the weather report before I set out; I had already walked a couple miles when it started to rain. Being several miles away from my own house, the only choice I really had was to reach my destination.

I remember trembling in my hands and feeling cold sweat in my palms as I approached her residence. I saw her coming out the front door. I ushered the words out of my mouth as she walked out, shocked by my presence. With one word falling over another, I asked her out the sloppiest and clumsiest way imaginable, but by some miracle she said yes.

At that moment, something clicked in me. It was that childish optimism, that unrealistic belief that I could do anything and be anyone, which I had suppressed after fifteen years of repeated failures in the educational world where you're reprimanded for every mistake you make. I then realized that our best chance of success comes after we are willing to fail. We have to attempt feats that might seem unrealistic. We have to attempt all those things that make us uncomfortable, that make us ache in our stomach. We have to be able to push ourselves to try and make an effort, even though all odds seem stacked against us. We have to attempt to walk through those rainy days when everything seems to be going downhill, when everything seems to be getting messy and not in our favor, but still look ahead to the sunshine.

> **We have to be willing to allow ourselves to try these things and fail at them, because the more we fail at them the more we learn.**

We have to be willing to allow ourselves to try these things and fail at them, because the more we fail at them the more we learn. We learn by analyzing what it is that we're doing that's not working. How can we do things differently for a better outcome? How we can use maximum effort and new, exciting ways to solve problems, to tackle tasks that are presented to us? Once we have dissected this analysis, we can begin to find the appeal in doing things our own way. We start attracting others to become more inquisitive and approach things that they thought were unrealistic. We inspire an If-You-Can-Do-It-So-Can-I type of mentality.

You will soon inspire others to approach life differently by becoming a person that has a sense of confidence, an air of willingness to fail while still figuring things out for yourself. You might not be an expert, but the fact that you are willing to attempt things that are just beyond your grasp, willing to fail at them, and able to analyze your results—not as failures, but as learnings— allows you to better enhance your next steps. This enhances your courage to try again and become better. When you are willing to fail, you are vulnerable. Being vulnerable allows you to

connect better with other people, and it allows you to connect better with your internal self, becoming your own best friend.

Being able to share intimate details of your life with your best and closest friend is a sign of vulnerability. That is exactly why they are your best and closet friend: because you are willing to be vulnerable with them. Having this vulnerability in trying unrealistic tasks and being willing to fail shows other people that you are someone of great capabilities. Once you've developed the willingness to attempt tasks and fail at them, you'll start developing tolerance for people who are trying their own ways, are maybe doing things a little differently, walking to the beat of a different drum. You start opening your own mind to the possibility that maybe other people can find better ways of doing something that you've always done another way. Maybe there are different ways to challenge the status quo. Maybe there are ways to maximize effort and efficiency without having to do the same things over and over.

We start to see that the different perspectives that people take come from mostly positive motives, and they truly want to make a positive impact. We might not see it that way at first, but as we begin to tolerate the different approaches of different people we can start to understand their motives. We start to understand where they're coming from, why they're doing this, and why they think this is good. We can then improve ourselves and others by communicating the differences in the styles, seeing what works and what doesn't, meshing them together to make sure they're in sync and our viewpoints are aligned. This improves not only us as individuals but also the team that we're part of, the people that we love, the people that we work with.

"INNOVATION DISTINGUISHES BETWEEN A LEADER AND A FOLLOWER."

STEVE JOBS

CHAPTER FIVE
CONFIDENT SELF

When I was in high school, I was heavily overweight due to a combination of financial hardship, a lack of awareness, and lack of exercise. I finally got sick of being overweight and unhealthy, so I decided to sign up for a personal fitness class in high school. I remember walking into the class and seeing everybody sitting around the weight room. Everybody else seemed to be in great shape—thin, fit, athletic people—and I felt like the black sheep.

The instructor, Coach Slive, soon came out of his office, sat down with us, and explained that in your current situation, you might not be able to run as fast as the guy next to you. You maybe can't lift as much weight as your classmate, but that doesn't stop you from lifting an extra five pounds. That doesn't stop you from taking up your game to the next level. That doesn't stop you from working an extra hour than everyone else to get to where you want to be. It definitely does not define who you will be in the future.

His words really resonated with me because I was sick and tired of being who I was. I felt trapped by the definition everyone else had placed on me. I felt like I was overweight permanently. This class and Coach Slive's help opened a door for me that led to my acceptance of my current self. It let me own up to who I was at the time, who I was because of this situation and the choices I had made. Finally being comfortable with myself allowed me to see myself through a new lens, to see myself clearly for who I was at the moment so that I could embrace the situation that I was in and take a step in a better direction. Once I was able to accept where I was in that moment, I could move forward and seek the beauty that was in my future. The best part about the future is that it has yet to happen—anything is possible. Every little choice that we make allows us to build the future according to our own path.

The biggest problem with building the future is that most people don't live in the present. Most people live either in the past or the future. The past can't be changed, so dwelling on it will only degrade the present moment with illusions of what could have been different. Living in the future isn't good either; when you live in a future that hasn't happened yet, a space that is only in your mind, it can detract from your actions in the present. Learn to exist in the present, where you can plan for the future, learn from the past, and take action to reach your goals. You can do so many things once you're in the present moment, and you dedicate yourself to practicing and improving what you're doing at the present rather than worrying about the past or future.

Yes, I sometimes focused too much on the future. I was impatient to be fit and athletic in the future I envisioned, whereas I was still overweight in the present. But when I owned up to my current status, I was able to take a step into that weight room every day we had class. I was able to take a step into our exercises, feel the bar in my hands, feel the exertion in my body, feel the growth and changes my body was going through. Soon the weight started coming off my body. Everything that happened in my transition was because I accepted present and dedicated myself to changing it, to practicing and exercising and going towards my vision of the future I wanted. I chose and defined the little steps that I was going to take in the present to get to where I want to go. This presence, tolerance, and acceptance of the current self gives us a fuel for our passion to become better.

Knowing the difference between where we are today and where we want to go tomorrow gives us a sense of urgency. Asking ourselves, "Where am I now? What do I need to get done tomorrow? How do I get from here to there?" helps us develop a plan to push ourselves to achieve the things that we want to achieve. Develop your own plan to obtain the future that you want with the sense of urgency because it is your time. It is your life, and you need to do this for yourself now.

In the quest to become better people, one of the most popular sayings to be passed down through generations is that practice makes perfect. Coaches all around the world insist on repetition and practice and repetition and practice. The thing about practice is that it must be dedicated. You have to be present in the practice and feel every little motion, every little gesture, that you are making in the practice. When you dedicate your mind to the practice you start picking up a lot of little stimuli that your brain might've passed by, deleted, or processed without your knowledge. The brain handles so many things on a daily basis, that there's no way it can consciously keep up with handling every little stimuli that comes in and every little detail. It has to resort to quick, unconscious methods of storing or

> **Asking ourselves "Where am I now? What do I need to get done tomorrow? How do I get from here to there?" helps us develop a plan to push ourselves to achieve the things we want to achieve.**

removing information that is not necessary.

When you are distracted or thinking about something else during practice, you start deleting those little details that may not feel important at the time but will be later. It's like when you're driving to work and all of a sudden you've arrived and you think to yourself, "Who was just driving? How did I get here?" This happens because you were thinking about something else, not focused on the task at hand, and your subconscious sorted this information without you noticing. It processed the unnecessary information and threw it out. The effect of dedicated practice combined with repetition is that you start noticing stimuli from the practice. That becomes a pattern in your head, which eventually can be moved through at quicker speeds. For example, we are able to calculate one plus one very easily because it's been drilled into our heads again and again. It has become a solid, locked down pattern in our heads. Once you begin to practice repeatedly with frequency a task that you want to improve upon, you will naturally start doing it faster and better after you consciously focus on what is happening when you practice. Even if you don't practice with dedication and you start doing a task repeatedly, mindlessly, much of the stimuli is filtered out and distraction

> **"This is where I want to go. This is what it's going to feel like. These are the things I'm going to hear. This is how I'm going to get there."**

is patterned into your head instead. So the next time you attempt the task, you start forgetting details, you start missing things. That's because you've patterned the carelessness into your brain, and it's associated with that task. Make sure you dedicate both your body and your mind to your practice.

After you have achieved enough repetition of a task, it will become easier and you will start to envision yourself more positively. For example, if you practice a sport and you advance in proficiency, you might start competing in district tournaments, then in state tournaments, then go on to national competitions. You will start seeing yourself as someone who is proficient in a certain task. You start viewing yourself positively in that domain. You start becoming an expert in that domain, one day at a time. Positive association with a task makes real to you. It becomes present. It's no longer the past. It's no longer the future. You

are proficient at this task. Having this positivity will give you an elevated level of confidence because you know you've done it before and you can do it again. Having this confidence and positivity in one aspect of your life can affect other parts of your life. Once you have a solid foundation of practice and dedicated learning you can start to branch out a little bit, start imagining even more things that you want in your future. Think about other paths that you'll want to take; explore them because once you have that foundation of development and growth, the proof of dedication and improvement, you can start actualizing other paths in your life. As unrealistic as your new goals might be, you can plan them out in your future, as long as you take actions in the present. As long as you commit to practicing hard, you will reach your goal.

Allow yourself to not only imagine but visualize yourself in these future paths. What would it look like if you had what you wanted? What would it feel like in the moment when you're receiving that award? What would it sound like when you're in the center and everyone is applauding for you? What would it be to you, as a person, as an individual, what would it mean to you? How would it change your being? This visualization of a new future combined with the positivity of your previous achievements will help you start to build a path to get there for yourself. You'll begin to talk with your best friend, yourself, your internal voice, and you chart out a treasure map. This is where I want to go. This is what it's going to feel like. These are the things I'm going to see. These are the things I'm going to hear and how we're going to get there is through this dotted line.

You begin to make your own path, one that fills you up with excitement, that makes you leap out of bed in the morning, because you know where you want to be, and you know the things you're going to see, the people you're going to have around you, the things you're going to do. That is what drives you, because it's fun to you. Once you are on that path, once you are on that mission, you will start to radiate positivity and confidence to other people, and they will want to help you too.

"CREATIVITY IS INTELLIGENCE HAVING FUN."

ALBERT EINSTEIN

CHAPTER SIX
APPLIED CREATIVITY

There is no better allegory for this chapter than the biggest catastrophe of my life thus far, which led me on the journey to become the best version of myself. It was an instance that involved two very beautiful people close to me. I ended up hurting both of them very deeply. Due to my poor communication skills and my lack of integrity at the time, I misconstrued the situation and my desires to both parties. When things started crashing down during this incident, I couldn't bear to accept the truth at the time. I couldn't look myself in the mirror and accept who I was: I was my own worst enemy. It was one of the darkest times of my life. Because I had these two wonderful people in my life, unfortunately it had to resort to tragedy for me to realize things weren't right.

To this day, the guilt from my actions drives me to make sure I am completely in line with my own values as well as seek out what it means to be a true person of integrity. I took it upon myself, although bad things had already happened, to start making changes so that this would never happen again, so that I wouldn't hurt the people that are important to me.

After extensive months of studying books and therapy sessions, I really began to understand these concepts of accepting oneself, building a fun persona, and becoming a success. I started to internalize each of these things one at a time. By no means did I fully internalize all of these concepts, but I have an awareness of them now and can apply them to my life. The revelation from this catastrophe piqued my curiosity as to what I can discover about my own character and how I can share my learnings with other people. It gave me a craving to become a man of integrity. It gave me a desire and a burning passion to be someone that others can rely on, and that I can count on my own decisions in times of desperation.

This craving led me to an extended period of exploration. I challenge you to have the same curiosity about the things that excite you in life. The things that you feel, deep down, you should be doing. The things that might make you scared to move forward and take action. Curiosity gives you the craving and passion that you need to start exploring options, to start looking for your own way to venture into the path that you desire most. Start listening to the craving and honing in on what it is that you want, what things that drive you, what things that make you want to tell your friends about. Create your own adventures. Progress where it is you want to be because in life, it's not about

where you end up, it's about the journey, the adventures that you go on, the people that you meet, the things that you see and the tales that you hear that really make you who you are. They embellish your strengths and assist you in becoming a better person, the oracle that others can look to. Having that foundation then building on your character gives you an aura of confidence.

Because you've been curious, you've been on these adventures, you are able to say, "I have the competence to go out and try the things that I always wanted to do." When you take steps to do new things, you will realize that you are capable, and you build competence. You will then begin to accept the fact that you have the flexibility to be a little creative, to be a little curious about the things you do in life, to go out a little bit out of the norm and do things your own way. You find paths that people don't walk as often. You will develop the flexibility to wiggle around and overcome the obstacles in your life—that's confidence: when someone is unafraid to handle any task because they have the flexibility to maneuver around obstacles, the competence to solve things, and the enthusiasm to try things that they have not done before.

Confident people also possess one more element, and that is cadence. They know from prior experience, from doing things over and over, from failing again and again and learning from all those experiences, that they have a cadence or rhythm in their behaviors. They know how fast they can travel, how many new adventures they can go on, how many obstacles they can handle at one time. Having that cadence to guide them along their new adventures or obstacles helps them to know how easily they can get around it. Once you have developed your own cadence, knowing how much you can handle, knowing that you can flex around obstacles and

problems, knowing that you can do things that are new and creative, you will exude a succinct aura of confidence that you can then share with others. When we have a confident leader, we become more confident ourselves. As social creatures, we all feed off of the confidence of our leader. When you can exemplify that confidence for your peers, you become a source of confidence, a source of leadership, and you empower those around you. People will gravitate to you. Confidence and curiosity assist you in building your character through your journeys. You will build a congruent and a consistent version of you that other people witness.

That version of yourself that is presented to others is who you would want to be, who you think you are; align it with who you want the world to see you as. Having this consistency allows others to become familiar with who you are much more rapidly. They will understand you better. You will understand yourself better. You start becoming your own best friend more consistently. You don't fight yourself on your own decisions because you know who you are, you know what you are going to do, and you know how you are going to do it.

Once you establish consistency, you must develop personal integrity. When you are consistent with yourself, when you are congruent with your decisions, when you have the confidence that you can maneuver around any obstacles and handle any new adventures and be curious and inquisitive about anything that's going on, you become a person of true integrity. You are able to stand behind every decision you make. You are able to understand this step, this leap of faith, towards this new adventure, and why you are being driven to do the things you want to do: because you are passionate about it, you have a craving for that adventure, for that path. It will take you to where you want to be in the future.

The next step of complete integrity is to follow through on those feelings. After you have gathered all of your confidence and curiosity to figure out where you want to go, all your congruence to keep you in line, you need to follow through on your step. You put one foot after your other, and that is how you get to where you want to be—one step at a time. You will soon become the ultimate optimized version of yourself, where you can have true meaning in your life, where you have fun doing the things that you do. At the same time, you inspire others to be great. You impact your community, and everyone around you notices that you are a person that exudes confidence and is congruent. You show that you are a person of integrity.

{ **"FUN IS GOOD."** }

DR. SEUSS

FUN LIFE: BUILDING A FUN LIFE THROUGH PRACTICE AND CREATING NEW OPPORTUNITIES FOR FUN

{ "no one looks stupid when they're having fun." }

AMY POEHLER

CHAPTER ONE
PUTTING FUN TO WORK

Recalling back to the end of my first long-term committed relationship, yet another painful experience, we were together for just over a year and three months. It was around April when we finally sat down and talked and got things squared away, laid out the terms, and agreed on just being friends and no further association. It was a rather horrible breakup, but it ended up working out for the better for both sides. I'm happy to say that we're friends now, and we even get together to play games on occasion.

It wasn't easy for me to break up with her at the time because in actuality, I was the problem in the relationship. Now, sharing all these stories might make me seem like a horrible person, and believe me, I was, but that just goes to show how much one can change if you put your heart and soul into working to grow and change. You own up to your inefficiencies and work on improving them.

My first steps toward change were breaking down the anatomy of our relationship. You can do the same to your current relationship, your job, anything that you feel is not working out for you. Scrutinize the elements of what is going on, what is working, what is not working, and why. Break down the anatomy to the point where you can identify each piece that is not working for you and find alternatives. You must either change those activities that are not working, remove them, or pass them on to someone else. That might entail leaving your current position to change to a different position. That might entail leaving your team to go to a different team. That is all dependent on your specific circumstances and requires a deeper understanding of what exactly is going on in your current role.

For me, I had to break down what was wrong in the relationship; I realized that I was not able to communicate emotionally. Because of that, resolutions were very difficult when we got to fights. I isolated that part that wasn't working, and I realized that I had to work on it. In that specific situation, it was the best option for me to remove that thing that wasn't working. I pulled myself out of the relationship and decided to fix and target that aspect of myself.

We have to, in this process, adopt new techniques, new methods, of approaching tasks. I had to find a way to communicate better. I took a class in romantic relation communications, and I started to learn about all these ways to start finally communicating my emotions and understand what others are feeling. Then I could better connect the way I wanted to with people. In your job, when you start isolating the things that aren't working for you, you can start to look for new venues of doing these tasks. You can look for a mentor or a coach that can guide you on different ways to approach your work. You can talk to your manager about changing the assignments to other people or shifting

> **"When we put our strengths first, when we put fun first and we apply it to our work, we start correcting the symptoms of employee disengagement."**

to a different role. When you begin to adopt new ways of handling these tasks that aren't working for you, you can alleviate your situation and allow yourself more room to work on your strengths, more room to have fun in your career. By focusing on the things that make you feel strong, by focusing on the things that make you excited, your attitude and therefore end results will improve.

When you're excited, you'll be more productive, leaving more space and time for you to focus on the tasks that are difficult and find new ways to handle them. You have to adjust your situations based on things that you're passionate about because focusing on tasks and things that make you feel strong will generate more excitement, energy, and passion within your daily activities. That energy and passion will spill over to other tasks in your life, to other activities, to other teammates, to other co-workers, and this in turn makes up for the tasks that you are less adept at.

Being exceptionally productive in the things that you do well allows you to build your own confidence. Remember that fun persona you just built; vitalize yourself, invigorate yourself, allow yourself to be the beacon that shines for other people. That gives an opportunity for others to reach out to you, to help you become better in the tasks that you're less adept at. In order to make this happen, we have to identify what our strengths are, what things make us excited, and what tasks we find fun and energizing. Some of this can be determined through personality tests or strength assessments—they can help you take a better look at yourself, understand what you're good at, and how you can implement the strategy of working around your weaknesses and magnifying your strengths.

When you work on your strengths, the things that you're great at, the things that excite you, you will multiply your productivity and results, rather than dwelling on the tasks that you're not so great at, the tasks that bog you down. When you spend time stuck in the tasks you're ill-equipped for, you lose produce across the map. You become less excited about your work. You become less engaged in your work. Not only does your productivity go down, your entire team feeds off your negative energy because you're not engaged in your work. That brings down productivity in your teammates as well.

When we put our strengths first, when we put fun first and we apply it to our work, we start correcting the symptoms of employee disengagement. We start correcting the problems of feeling overwhelmed, feeling overworked, and waking up without energy because when we feel energized, we start fixing these little feelings of not being alive. When we are able to talk to ourselves freely about things that we want to do, new ways to tackle the problems that we want to handle, we have more time and energy to handle the problems that we are inclined to deal with. We can be more creative in finding different ways to overcome those problems, navigate around them, have the flexibility to pawn them off to another teammate who might be great at them and allow him or her to shine and bring your productivity up just as much as you do with them by being more excited about your work.

"IF YOU OBEY ALL THE RULES, YOU MISS ALL THE FUN."

KATHERINE HEPBURN

CHAPTER TWO
PREPARING TASKS AND DUTIES WITH FUN

At the beginning of college, I was invited to a party. As a first year college student, I was mandated by all unwritten collegiate laws to attend a party. My roommates and I went out to the party and were having a great time—I was simply crowd-watching in the party, enjoying my cup of water when all of a sudden, a lady reaches her hand out to me and asks me to dance. I froze because I had no idea how to dance, but I went on the floor anyway and we danced. We ended up going outside to talk for a while. It was a very nice conversation. Before I knew it, I had her number, and she was gone.

The next night, after I had gotten back from yet another night of partying—as again mandated by all collegiate law—I sent her a text message because I was grateful for her showing me how to dance. It didn't occur to me that it was about 2:00 in the morning. A few minutes later, she responded, "Okay, I'm up."

"What do you mean?" I asked, confused.

"Well, I'm up now, and meet me in front of your dorm in 10 minutes," she said.

I said, "Okay," and went out to meet with her.

When I brought her to the lobby of my dormitory, it suddenly occurred to me that this was a booty call: if you text somebody of the opposite gender at 2 a.m. on a Saturday night, you are expressing potential sexual interest. This was my first booty call. I didn't know that was how it was going to go down, but we sat in the lobby and chatted for a couple hours.

Most people think of fun as being leisurely downtime. However, if you think of it that way, you fail to understand the effects of how energized fun can enhance your productivity and creativity. When you are having fun, dopamine chemicals are released in your brain— it is very powerful in encouraging energized fun behavior. When you start incorporating fun into your planning, into your activities, even in work, you start enhancing your experiences. Studies have shown that when you have more humor at work, you are more engaged in your job and actually produce more results by spending a little downtime chatting humorously with your co-workers.

When we start to understand that having fun when we're planning new things, when we're approaching new tasks, can help us identify the ways that we are empowered by it. We notice just how much more we can get done when we are having fun in our approach to our business, to our tasks, to our chores. I encourage you to approach tasks and think in ways that excite you and try things in ways that you enjoy.

For example, when you go out on a date and everything is already planned, you're only going to have as much fun as you get out of those specific activities. But what if you take a little bit of a different approach? Maybe you go out and arrange a set block of time to do one planned activity, then the rest of the time is up to you to be spontaneous. It will allow you and your date with to come together in a different and unique approach, to try to come up with something that's exciting and fun for both of you on the spot. It might be very challenging at first, but with enough practice, I'm sure you and your partner can navigate and have a blast at the same time throughout the entire process.

I encourage you to practice new methods, to decide how you're going to respond to a task, to decide on your own creative decisions. Just try them out. Commit to them and act on them because the greatest people in life do things out of their own excitement and passion. They create things, and they commit to them, and they act on making them real before they even share it with the world. When you create things and they don't work out, then there's always room for remediation, learning, and new possibilities. If you never act on your own creative ideas, if you never innovate, if you never do things that excite you and you find fun, then you start living a life that's not really alive. You start becoming part of the living dead. You do mundane things. You do things that don't excite you. You do them because you think you have to. You do them because you have bought into the idea that your dreams are not as imperative as your need to be what others say you are.

> **Decide on what makes your day more vivid, more colorful, and commit to doing one little thing about it a day.**

Decide on what makes your day more vivid, more colorful, and commit to doing one little thing about it a day. Not everyone can handle the amount of risk or uncertainty that comes with taking a huge leap, but if you take a small step in a thousand-step journey every single day, you're going to get closer to your goal. Decide on a tiny step each day, commit to a small portion of the task, and then act on getting to where you need to go, getting to where you feel you should be going, getting to where your heart tells you to go. You'll get there if you keep stepping.

"WORK IS MORE FUN THAN FUN."

NOËL COWARD

CHAPTER THREE
PRESENTING IN A FUN FASHION

When I came on board as a specialist in acquisition for my real estate firm, I was given the general idea of how to go about conducting appointments. I was given examples by riding along and observing others' appointments. However, I was soon given the free reign to choose exactly how I was going to present myself and how I was going to connect with the customers. Having this free reign allowed me to push my own agenda alongside the agenda of the firm and accomplish much that went beyond anyone's expectations. As a result, I got the nickname of "Golden Child," or GC for short.

This really reinforced in me the idea of putting our own fun spin on presentations, putting our own twists on the status quo, and modifying the current system to help us, to make things easier for us and the people that we're delivering our presentations to. We shouldn't feel afraid to disrupt the current system a little bit, to improve our odds at achieving our goal, and to enhance our presentation to the other parties. When we feel the desire to do something differently, to present a little more stylistically or to put our own creative spin on our presentations, but shut that down out of fear or obligation, we turn our heads away from fun and away from ourselves. If we simply go along with the system, even though we know that we can do it differently and better, then we are being inconsistent with ourselves. We start fighting our own internal voice, our own instincts, which separates us from being our own best friend.

Just like with any friend, if you have a disagreement on opinion, there might be a little tenser conflict than usual. There might be some ruffling of emotions. You must allow yourself to put your own spin on things; go ahead and disrupt the current system so long as you are keeping track of whether or not it is working. As long as you are freely and accurately delivering the information, feel free to dream a little bit of an ideal presentation style for yourself. When you have an outline of what you want your presentations to look like, what you want your audience to respond to, you can go ahead and implement those actions. Decide how you're going to present so that you'll elicit the response you're your audience that you want. You'll be able to convey the message that your audience is ready to hear.

Put your own creative flair on your work so that it emphasizes the parts that you want people to pay attention to. If we allow ourselves the opportunity and deliberation to change the presentation style in our favor, we can begin to receive feedback for how much effort we're putting in, how much our style impacts the results as opposed to the current system style. In fact, you might find something that someone else wasn't able to see before.

There are three E's to remember for adding your own flair to presentations: envision, enlighten, and entertain. We begin by envisioning how we want this presentation to proceed and how we want the audience to respond. In what ways will we have fun while conveying this message and allowing this audience to feel us? After we have a solid vision of what is going to happen, what we're going to see and hear, we can then plan out how we are going to convey our message properly so that it enlightens the other parties. The other parties should understand what we're trying to share after we understand what they are looking to receive. Once we have this mutual understanding, presentations become automatic and free-flow, which allows us to become a lot more receptive and responsive as well as effective. When things are free-flow, it is significantly easier for us to entertain our audience. When we can understand where they're coming from, we can communicate on a level of friend-to-friend and ally-to-ally. They become a lot more receptive to any ideas that we choose to throw at them, to entertain our thoughts and beliefs and the service that we are offering.

I encourage you to take a look at the presentations you're doing at your daily job in person or on paper. Take a look at the opportunities you have to speak in front of someone, and think about how you would ideally represent the issue. Think about what you want your audience to see, how you

want them to feel, and what kind of responses would you like to hear from them. How can you make that presentation more entertaining for yourself? How can you make that more exciting for you your audience? How can you add your own twists to

> **"**
> **There are 3 E's to remember for adding your own flair to presentations:**
> ## • envision
> ## • enLiGHTen
> ## • enTeRTAIn.
> **"**

the presentation and give it its own color, thereby making your audience more receptive?

{ YOU GOTTA HAVE FUN. REGARDLESS OF HOW YOU LOOK AT IT, WE'RE PLAYING A GAME. IT'S A BUSINESS, IT'S OUR JOB, BUT I DON'T THINK YOU CAN DO WELL UNLESS YOU'RE HAVING FUN. }

DEREK JETER

CHAPTER FOUR
FINDING AND PLANNING FUN ACTIVITIES

One time I was on vacation and decided to take an extra few days than planned to really enjoy the getaway. I didn't know the area very well, so I went online and I did some research. I found some local tourist attractions and decided I would connect with some locals to see if they would be willing to take me there. It turned out to be one of the best vacations of my life because I was able to explore the area through the perspective of natives. They gave me an in-depth understanding of the history behind the attractions and the local stories.

I wouldn't have had such a great experience if I hadn't looked up some places to go and took the initiative to ask someone who knew the area better to guide me through the locations. The same is true for daily life. When we're looking for local activities, when we're looking for something interesting to do around town, we can go online and look for tourist attractions or activities nearby, even look on applications that offered discounts to local activities. Once we find activities to take part in, we can reach out to the establishment or group with a phone call so that we establish a connection. That's important because in today's world, most people are looking at things online, booking things through email or other electronic formats, and people are losing that human-to-human connection. When you reach out and you call the host of the event or the company that is hosting the activity, you establish yourself as a real person. That gives you an edge on discounts, on attendance, on different time slots, and any flexibility they have in their schedule.

Now, bringing people to activities is also one of the most crucial elements to making sure that when you find some activity around town, it becomes a very exciting and fun event. We naturally bond with others through an activity, whether it be positive bonding or negative bonding. Regardless of the situation, you will end up with a more exciting story. This is also why laughter is more frequent when others are nearby. Our emotions are heightened. Our excitement is heightened. When you invite people to activities, you start becoming a person of interest in the

> **Laughter is more frequent when others are nearby; our emotions are heightened. Our excitement is heightened.**

sense that you create interesting opportunities for people to get together. You create ways for people to improve their own social circle, to do something different. By doing so, you start becoming a person of interest in not only business, but also in relationships and friendships.

The more people you invite to an activity, the better, but you might be thinking that the cost of hosting a fun activity would be too much to handle. Surprisingly, if you do some research about local activities hosted by local or mobile units, you will find that it cost a lot less than you might imagine, especially if you book big group events. There are usually discounts for events with lots of people, usually over a certain number. When you shop around and you compare prices, you can again call the event sponsors and see if there are any price comparisons or any offer they can give you for big groups. Usually local events want your business and are willing to negotiate and work with you to make sure that you are getting the best deal possible.

Make sure that your group agrees on a payment, either after you finish the activity or when you're paying for the activity. If it's at all possible, pay the establishment or company a little more than agreed upon because once you start building a relationship with that person or company, it will be more likely and a lot easier for you to get looped in on discounts and other exciting activities that go on. It's better to build a longer lasting relationship with that sponsor. Maybe they'll do something special for you next time, and you'll have a better connection with local event hosts. That will allow you more opportunity for exciting events later on.

IDEAS FOR LOCAL ACTIVITIES TO HOST

- **Go-Karting**
- **Archery Tag**
- **Escape Room**
- **Social Group Ballroom Dance Lessons**
- **Aerial Yoga**
- **Improv Shows**
- **Bubble Soccer**
- **Whitewater Rafting**
- **Board Game House Party**

"IF YOU'RE NOT HAVING FUN IT'S NOT WORTH DOING."

TOMMY BOLIN

CHAPTER FIVE

PACKING FUN FOR THE ROAD

I remember when I rode my very first roller coaster. Ever since I was little, I'd had a terrifying phobia of heights. It wasn't until I got into my few sessions of hypnotherapy that I was able to put myself into a roller coaster and just let go, let myself have a ball on this ride, because there was nothing else I could do except enjoy the moment. That's what it's like when you're on the road.

When you're out and about, you have to utilize your creativity and live in the present moment. You're away from your comfortable home, your computer, your game station, all the distractions that are usually able to find you at home, so you have nothing better to do than to focus on your present moment and the people you're with. During these times, you're forced to use your creativity. Why not use it for fun and exciting things rather than dwelling on what you could be doing instead or what isn't going right?

One of the easiest ways to do this is to simply anticipate events during your upcoming trip. Think about how magnificent something would be, about the small aspects that could amuse you instead of what might go wrong. "What if's" can be used for good instead or for bad. When you are your own best friend, nothing feels greater than to imagine and anticipate all the wonderful possibilities of what is to come on this trip.

Once you have that presence of mind, implement your creative imagination and consider what could happen and what you could do on this trip. You can start to ideate and think about things that you would like to do on the trip. Think about the kind of fun that you want to have, something that you've been dying to do, and how do you make that happen. Make sure that the company you're with understands that you are excited about something because maybe something that you're excited about is not something that they are. As much as they want you to have fun on this trip, as much as they want you to be excited and energetic on this trip, they might not know that specific event or task is what would enable you to be at your fullest potential. Make sure you share your ideas and imaginations and desires so that you and your company as a whole can create these experiences.

When you do the things that you are excited about and have fun with on this journey, you start to lose track of all the stress and distractions that may have been with you earlier. This allows your mind to relax, settle back, and feel alive again. When you create space for yourself and others around you to have fun, to be excited about life, you create a space for your mind to rejuvenate itself. It will end up being more productive when you return. There is an efficiency technique that calls for 30 minutes of productivity followed by 5 minutes of rest. The short spurts cause excitement and focus, and allows an individual to be highly productive and not be overwhelmed.

The key part of instilling great fun and excitement in your journey is the imagination that you bring with you. If you have a vivid, clear, imaginative task and you share that with others, you instill clarity in the minds of others. When you can picture exactly what it is you want to do, exactly what kind of things will excite you, you allow others to join you on your journey, to join you on your anticipation of what's to come. Having this picture depicted in vivid detail for you and your friends allows everyone to be on the same page and have fun together.

The experience of being bonded together enraptures human beings because we are social creatures. We are herd animals, having a common goal and common vision. Having that clarity of the picture of fun and exciting tasks that are ahead allows everyone to be united and feel even closer as a unit. This elevates the fun and excitement in everybody and intensifies all forms of productivity. This is the perfect time to capture that productivity and use it for not only creating long-lasting memories, but also uncovering creative ideas that would have been brushed aside before.

Take conferences or conventions, for example. People get riled up; their passions and motivations are excited, and they're able to accomplish so much in just a few days. When they go back to normality, they might falter a little bit because their passion subsides. But if your vision is clear enough, if you are united with yourself, with your peers, and with your company, you'll be able to take the actions to stay on the path, to take that glory home with you and use it to keep pushing on.

> **"** When you create space for yourself and others around you to have fun, to be excited about life, you create a space for your mind to rejuvenate itself. **"**

"I never did a day's work in my life. It was all fun."

THOMAS EDISON

CHAPTER SIX
PUSHING FOR THE FUN

As mentioned previously, I was very socially inhibited during high school. In order to finally get some social interaction and get some relief of my social alienation, I decided to pick up magic. I chose to focus on street magic, so that I could learn to perform in close proximity with others. Then I could go anywhere, talk to anybody, perform right in front of them, and have an excuse to have a conversation. Some might think it was quite pathetic, but it worked for me.

I remember there was this one technique that was so fascinating to me when I saw it. I was so proud of myself when I came up with a way to go about performing the technique. I later found out, unfortunately, that the way I was doing it was not the way I'd actually been taught. Despite this, the results were the same, and, in fact, I got phenomenal responses from my audience. They loved the way I performed it, even though they had no idea it was not the same as the way I had been taught.

This made me realize that I don't have to perform the way that others do. If I get the same results, I get the point across in a unique way, and I create a special experience for my audience, then who is to say that my way is wrong? Why is it wrong to be different? It became clear that when we discover our own way of doing things, and we perform them confidently, it becomes right in every sense of the method. As long as you're getting the proper message across to your audience, and your audience is completely satisfied, then there is no difference in what you should be doing.

This all boils down to having faith in your own abilities. Everyone has different learning styles, different strengths. Even though they may all be different, they're all right—everyone has a unique contribution to the group. Because of those differences, they're able to make the group that much better. Discover your own way of doing things, your own unique contribution to your social group. When you have faith in your own abilities, you exemplify a unique sense of confidence. You allow other people to become more self-reliant, more self-empowered, and more excited to find their own path, their own way of doing things that will benefit the group at the same time.

Once you've found this structure that you can use to deliver the results that you've been looking for, you have essentially created magic. Magic is really the difference between having a structure that works, and showing results without people knowing exactly what the process is—however you do it, however you deliver the result, whatever structure you use. As long as people can see the result and they can see it done successfully again, and again, it is magical. The audience might not know what you're doing or how you're doing it, but the fact that you can repeatedly generate these results is in fact magical by definition.

> **When you are able to use your own fear of failure to drive yourself forward and deliver your own methods, then you are being a very courageous person.**

In order to do this effectively, we must call upon the courage that we developed in the previous chapters by being vulnerable and willing to fail. We have to channel this courage to push our own structures forward out into the public. We have to use this courage that we've developed to move our own beliefs into the public's eye. You will be criticized, and you will be judged. That's all part of the process, so don't let fear stop you. There will always be that fear of failure. Courage is not the lack of fear; courage is being afraid of the right things at the right time. When you are able to use your own fear of humiliation or failure to drive yourself forward and deliver your own discoveries, your own methods, then you are being a very courageous person.

However, if you let fear stop you, you're becoming no more than the person who gave up. You're becoming no more than what you were yesterday. By staying the same, you're actually declining in society. By not growing, and not pushing yourself to become more advanced, to become a better person, to challenge your own discoveries,

then you will not be able to persevere in today's fast-paced society. Because you're not growing, you will start to die a little bit inside because you're suppressing your own instincts, you're suppressing your gut feeling, your gut desire of fun. You start tearing away at becoming your own best friend. You start fighting with yourself again. That is when your confidence will shatter, and your courage starts falling away. This downward spiral is how people lapse into dark periods of self-doubt, and it all starts with fear.

Don't be afraid that you might not know the right answers or become an expert right away. Being an expert at something does not mean you have to know everything inside and out. Being great at something actually entails a lot of contradiction. For example, when you are a master of kung fu, you have to be able to be relaxed while at the same time tensing up to strike. You have to learn how to pull back and still maintain forward pressure. There are a lot of contradictions that, at first glance, might seem impossible to do or even unrealistic. Once you really take a deep look, you start to understand the little nuances behind the cover. Like when an acrobat needs to be relaxed on a bar, they also need their muscles to be tense to maintain their balance. When an expert practices their material, they are no more 100% understanding of the material than anyone else who has been practicing for several years. They have learned ways to be comfortable with the contradictions. They have learned ways to handle the differences. They've learned ways to test themselves.

Experts are able to identify areas where they're unbalanced. When they have too much consistency, they become rigid. When they don't have enough consistency, they become irresponsible. These experts have found tests and measures to keep themselves balanced, to find the right amount of consistency and the right amount of flexibility, so that they are adaptable and open-minded. These are tiny learnings that can make a world of difference in someone's career or life. When you learn how to have fun, and yet be able to handle business tasks, that is when your career will skyrocket. When you have too much fun, you seem lackadaisical. When you don't have enough fun, too much business mindset and focus, you seem hardheaded, almost unapproachable. When you mix the two together and strike the perfect balance, people will see your passion, your excitement, your focus, and your drive. They will be more inclined to follow you wherever you lead. Mastery is truly as grasping the art of oxymoron.

{ **"I HAVE FUN AT WORK."**

CAROL KANE }

FUN WITH OTHERS: INFLUENCING OTHERS WITH FUN LEADERSHIP AND INSPIRING OTHERS TO BE FUN LEADERS AS WELL

"A BUSINESS HAS TO BE INVOLVING, IT HAS TO BE FUN, AND IT HAS TO EXERCISE YOUR CREATIVE INSTINCTS."

RICHARD BRANSON

CHAPTER ONE
InFLuence WITH FuN

When I was in middle school I was a very disengaged student because I transferred from a very intense and rigorous school system to a public school system that didn't demand as much effort and dedication from their students. I became very detached from the public school system and I did the minimal amount of work to get by as I could. This meant that in every single class, I would sleep. I couldn't even try to pay attention through doodling because I wasn't good at it, so I just slept in all my classes. One of my teachers, a very bright man, was an excellent lawyer before he retired to be a teacher of Civics. He noticed that I was incredibly adept at answering all the questions when our class would play Jeopardy. I was engaged and would blow the others away with quick responses. I knew the material very well. However, in class when we weren't playing games, I was disengaged. I was tucked away in the corner, just dozing off and doing my own thing.

He pulled me aside one day and he said, "John, you're actually really far ahead of everyone else in the class." This caught my attention because I resonated with it. What he had taught me, after several more conversations, is that I can use my talents for good if only I would redirect my effort. He instilled that understanding in me by reaching out to me and finding out what it was that excited me, what it was that made me feel like I was having fun. He demonstrated different ways of having fun and enjoying myself that were more cohesive with what other students were doing in the class. He didn't force anything on me; instead, he led by example in doing things that he felt were fun. He paid attention to what exactly it was that resonated with me. When you become a leader, the essence of leading other people is to give them clarity.

When you are honed in on exactly how an activity can excite somebody, when you are focused on how to use something that is fun to you and show other people how you have fun doing it, you naturally give them a clear picture of what they can do as well, how they can find their own clarity through the way that you are executing a certain behavior. Being able to demonstrate something that is exciting and fun allows you to encourage collaboration amongst other people. This brings people together to generate this fun and exciting energy because humans innately want to enjoy being in the presence of others. When they see that they have an avenue for expressing this connected entertainment, when they have this feeling of united enjoyment, they are more likely to come together and work together to make it happen.

By allowing people to have these ways of becoming free and energized in participation, you start motivating other people to join in as well. It's like the one man that stands up and dances out in the crowd alone, and everyone is watching him. He is having a blast on the dance floor that he made for himself. People see how much joy he is having, so someone else joins in, and someone else joins in. Because he showed others how to have fun, how to enjoy the moment, he made other people to want to collaborate with him and join him on the dance floor that he made. As more people join in, other people are motivated to participate as well. Maybe not everyone is into dancing per se, many will participate by simply clapping or nodding their heads—most if not everyone starts participating because of the charismatic way that the first person showed others how to have fun.

Creating a fun and productive space is the essence of leadership. People are so bombarded with stress and responsibilities in today's fast-paced world that everyone suppresses their ability to have fun on a daily basis, thinking they will get more accomplished without it. Being able to step up and show others how to have fun again, how to let loose gives them clarity on how they can lose some of that stress, how they can get away from that life even just for a little bit, and immerse back into the present moment without of all the worries and the future concerns.

As you step up and illustrate for others things that excite you, things that are fun for you, you'll start to realize that success in business is coming to you because you're doing things in a way that is fun to you. Other people will notice that. You're being rewarded with attention and people are gravitating toward you because you exude fun. Months or years down the road, when that magnetism that you've developed becomes a lifestyle, when you are a fun person to be around, you'll notice that you're involved in quite a few activities that are enjoyable. The connections you made back today when you went out and you made an extra effort to find fun activities, when you put in the hard work to really try to put your own creative spin on things, are finally paying off. This

> **As you step up and illustrate for others things that excite you, things that are fun for you, you'll start to realize that success in business is coming to you because you're doing things in a way that is fun.**

was the day that you made a difference.

The fact that you changed your lifestyle one step at a time, one step every day, allowed you to transform into the magnetic and attractive person that you have become. This is the kind of leadership that we should be aiming for. A kind of leader that can give others clarity, that can give others a future of hope, fun, and excitement, and can give a clear direction that instills some order in our lives and allows us to shed some of the chaos. A good leader helps others to become present in the moment and feel alive again. The best way to do that is through exemplary behavior. Some of the greatest leaders today are the ones who own their lives, who take the necessary actions to put their own spin on things, to disrupt the status quo, to make sure that people in their vicinity are able to see the vision that they have created for themselves, to see how much they love doing what they're doing.

"LIVE AND WORK BUT DO NOT FORGET TO PLAY, TO HAVE FUN IN LIFE AND REALLY ENJOY IT."

EILEEN CADDY

CHAPTER TWO
innovate with fun

When I first came to the United States, I was eight years old and I spoke one word of English. I knew how to say, "No," but I didn't even understand what it meant. I went to school and the very first thing the teacher asked me after a long spiel of gibberish to me at the time was, "Do you understand?" At the time I didn't know what that phrase meant, but it quickly became familiar to me because she said it to me again, and again, and again every single day. Whenever I would say, "No" in response to "Do you understand?" I was put on a side of the classroom or in the back onto a little, beige, picnic cloth. Then she pulled out a large bin of Legos and I got to play with them all day.

Even though I learned English in about a month, I pretended to not understand. I faked my way through an entire year and a half of school just so I could play with Legos all day in class because it didn't seem fun to me to participate in the classroom activities. But one day in 3rd grade, I accidentally quoted a phrase from a movie. I didn't know any better at the time that one of the words was a curse word. The little boy I said it to, in great humor, tattled on me, and I was busted for knowing how to speak and understand English. My Lego days ended.

Nonetheless, I learned the valuable lesson of being playful in my mannerism and to allow myself to have a playful mindset that attempts odd things or tries something a little out of the ordinary. When we are playful in life, and we are accepting of different circumstances of different people, we come across many solutions that are unorthodox but maybe work twice as well. We discover solutions that we didn't think of but someone else on the other side of the fence thought of. We come across memories and events that surprise us from everything that we've ever been taught. Harnessing these experiences and this playfulness allows us to venture into unknown territories, to expand our sphere of understanding.

When we have an empowered understanding of life, by being adventurous and owning our playfulness, we start to develop new ways of solving problems and we start to make connections that we otherwise would not have. It allows us to not only enhance our own spirituality and really connect with ourselves in that we are having fun and doing the things we want to, but we also allow others into our lives. We enhance our connections and networks so that we may one day call on someone else to be creative with and tackle problems that you would not be able to do alone, or call on that friend that you made while you were accidentally trying something new and made a fool of yourself and you both laughed your rears off.

Being able to adopt a playful attitude requires us to utilize our creativity, to bounce ideas off of current situations, and to attempt new things that might fail. The fun persona that you have developed, being willing to fail, being vulnerable and not pretending to be okay with the status quo, allows you to become a more powerful person. You can come up with new possibilities that you wouldn't have if you had admitted and accepted fate to run your life. The world wouldn't be what it is today if people like Nicola Tesla and Elon Musk chose to accept the status quo. They challenged their situations and the way things were done.

Once we have bounced our ideas around, we always have the option to change our minds, change our choices, and try something else. We're not stuck in the decisions that we make because when we are able to own up to our failures; we're putting our playfulness to use, and we are trying out new ways of doing things consistently, so we become adaptable and flexible. We can then quickly reset ourselves to make new decisions and tackle problems in a new method. It is important to try new projects, to do new tasks that you haven't done before because when you are trying to get from point A to point B, what got you there might not be the most effective or efficient. You might need to switch to a different vehicle. You might need to switch to a different type of tire to tread through the different terrain, to handle the different obstacles on the course.

> **When we have an empowered understanding of life, by being adventurous and owning our playfulness, we start to develop new ways of solving problems.**

When you try a new project, you also pick up new skill-sets. You find new teammates that might be able to do things that you weren't able to do before. You might learn techniques that enhance the way you are able to complete tasks. You can then collaborate on future actions more effectively, enhance that cadence that you're building. Find out how you are able to handle more obstacles and challenges coming your way and change your mind-set from that of a victim to that of a growth instead of complaining and being burdened by the obstacles that are pushing you down. The way of business is holding you back from finding new venues for you to put in your creativity, to push forward and try something new, to calibrate your own skills after reassessing what you've learned and taking your own success to the next level. Try something new. Use a different technique. Take on a different project and assess how you are doing compared to before. Is it working better than when you were following those strict routines? Is this something that is more effective for you? How are you coming across to people that you are working with? Finding new ways to do things inspires your own creativity as well as increase the motivation of others around you.

"WORK HARD. make money. HAVE FUN."

SAL GRECO

CHAPTER THREE
IMPACT WITH FUN

As mentioned in the beginning of this book, a good college friend of mine gave me a book that led me to learn how to speed read. It was also a book that taught, very simply, how to obtain mastery. It was one of the driving factors in my personal development. It helped me to hone in on what exactly it was that I wanted to do in life: I wanted to actualize the things that excited me. I am where I am today because of all the people in my life that shed some light on my life and gave me the opportunity to shine in theirs. What really gets me excited is finding a way to share my message with other people; to expand on the learnings, on the light, that others have shone upon my life; to really find the elements that make all these learnings true to me, and hash out all the details, so that I can compress all the details into a cohesive message that I can deliver to other people. To me, being able to take a vast amount of information and condense into concise and understandable terms is true mastery.

Find a message that you want to deliver in life. Find that tune that sounds perfect to you. The amount of fun you're going to have trying to expand upon that message, trying to find out all the details that you need in order to compress that message appropriately, will exponentially increase the success you have in your life. When you find the opportunity for you to contribute to something beyond your own development, to something beyond your personal gains, you transcend into a level of spirituality that no one can ever give you. You start to understand that being able to pass on your learnings to others is one of the greatest feelings in the world. It gives you the ability and desire to enhance the lives of others, whether that be people that are very near and dear to you, or people halfway across the globe. Whoever may be your audience, instilling a sensation of motivation in them, a new perspective, gives them that small advantage in renewing their lives. It affords a reward of incredible joy, indescribable happiness.

Having such a revelation in life—improving yourself to become a better person of integrity, into someone who is able to share some of their learnings with other people so they too can climb out of that dark space that they're in—is what drives me to dream every day. To share my learnings because I want to be the keeper of the light in the dark space I came from. I dream of the day when I can lead other people to more fun and exciting lives and change their world for the better one step at a time, one action at a time, one word at a time.

> **Find a message that you want to deliver in life. Find that tune that sounds perfect to you. The amount of fun you're going to have trying to expand that message will exponentially increase the success you have in your life.**

"IT'S KIND OF FUN TO DO THE IMPOSSIBLE."

WALT DISNEY

CHAPTER FOUR
INSPIRE WITH FUN

It wasn't until recently that I could look myself in the mirror and smile at myself for being my own best friend. I declared myself my closest ally instead of my closest enemy, that I love myself for who I am today. I'm not anywhere near perfect, and I don't believe I have everything that I want at the moment, but I'm still on my own journey. I've come to terms through enough development, understanding, and connections with my own instincts, that I know whenever I make a decision, I mean it. I can start believing in my choices because I know I am becoming a man of integrity.

Having that internal congruence and that identity of self-acceptance allows me to be more energetic in my day-to-day approach to life. It allows me to collect myself and choose where I want to use my energy. I can choose release my energetic vibes to crowds whenever they need a little oomph in their day, to find a stranger and give them a smile. I'm able to get up on rainy days and explode out of bed, feeling excited and energetic for the day that is to come. Instead of just being the recipient of a great day, I can intentionally make it a great day. You can do the same when you internalize the concepts of having fun in your choices, having fun in your life, and doing things that excite you. Exciting yourself will then excite those around you.

Once you're able to make choices that excite you, just go with it. Don't second guess yourself; simply attempt and attack with your chosen strategy. It may not be perfect. It doesn't have to be absolute. You can change and adapt because as consistent as great leaders are, they're also open-minded and adaptive. They can respond to problems as they come up. They can flex around the obstacles that come at them. If you attempt something new and it doesn't work, you know how to change your approach. You know what you have to do to avoid making the same mistake. When you start owning your own choices, when you start picking, and doing, and learning, you start to think and speak in a consistent manner that aligns with your internal values. This is when you become a greater level of yourself.

Most people today are too busy worrying about what others think of them. As Warren Buffet says, "An outer scorecard is what bogs people down. When you have an inner scorecard, when you care more about what you think of yourself, how you connect with yourself, you are efficient on levels that others cannot comprehend, in ways that exceed expectations." When you worry about what you think of yourself rather than what others think, and you follow through on the paths that you feel right, you become a person of integrity. Once you have integrity with yourself,

> "When you worry about what you think of yourself rather than what others think, then you become a person of **INTEGRITY.**"

you can begin to inspire it in others and cause a ripple of truth, love, leadership, and empowerment to those around you, to those near and dear to you, and even to those who might hear of you halfway across the world.

I challenge you to take the step back and reread the contents of this small book so that you may practice along with the steps and apply parts of it. As you develop a greater understanding, you can take the next step in finding a way to combine your personal persona through action by working with a professional, an expert, in self-mastery and fun.

I encourage you, after you've gone through the material in this book at least twice, to reach out to us and perhaps even participate in one of our live events. Although the material in the live event is very similar to the material covered in the book, the amount of energy that is shared with the people at the live event instills a different sense of purpose within each person. When many people gather for the same purpose—to have fun, to maximize their success, to take the world to the next level—a new group of leaders is created, a new aura of integrity and empowerment. Our live event internalizes all these concepts, physiologically, so that we create fun people, fun leaders, out of the building blocks you bring. Check us out at www.paralimus.com. And if nothing else, join the "Your Kungfu Mind" group on Facebook to snag some freebies on training your mind to be a grandmaster. I look forward to hearing from you.

"IF A MAN NEVER ALLOWED HIMSELF A BIT OF FUN, HE WOULD GO MAD."

HERODOTUS

JOHN HUI

ABOUT THE AUTHOR

WHO AM I?

A business success coach with extensive training in facilitation, peer communication, and sales. I created a new way of generating business impact by drawing from unique, yet overlapping, elements of kungfu, mindfulness, and sales. It is my firm belief that my life has been embellished by the light others have shown me while I was growing up, so coaching is my way of paying it forward.

www.paralimus.com

YOUR KUNGFU MIND
www.facebook.com/groups/894845247308326

{ **FUN** }

noun

: someone or something that is amusing or enjoyable

: an enjoyable experience or person

: an enjoyable or amusing time

: the feeling of being amused or entertained